Introduction

This book supports students preparing for the SQA Advanced Higher Mathematics examination. Written by experienced practitioner and mathematician, this comprehensive set of practice papers offers thorough preparation for the SQA assessment. Each practice paper is in line with the SQA syllabus and exam board specifications, and provides a rich and varied practice to meet all requirements of the SQA Advanced Higher Mathematics.

Papers are designed to teach students applicable, reusable and faster solutions to common problems. Each paper utilises problems to target areas of mathematics which students often find more difficult in the exam. Solutions provided have been reviewed by many students to ensure that they are easily understandable while being the fastest and most re-applicable.

The practice papers cover the following seven distinct topics:
1. Calculus
2. Algebra
3. Proof
4. Number theory
5. Matrices
6. Vectors
7. Complex numbers

After completing these practice papers, you should be able to:
1. Formulate optimal solutions quicker to any SQA Advanced Higher Mathematics question
2. More readily apply previously learnt skills on a question to question basis

The SQA Advanced Higher Mathematics practice papers comprises of 2 books, non-calculator and calculator, for Papers 1 and 2 in the SQA, respectively. Each book contains 4 full practice papers. For the book with calculator, each practice paper contains 13 questions and solutions. The non-calculator book contains 8 questions and solutions per paper.

Contents

1	Instructions	1
2	Paper 1	2
3	Paper 2	5
4	Paper 3	10
5	Paper 4	15
6	Paper 1 solutions	19
7	Paper 2 solutions	22
8	Paper 3 solutions	27
9	Paper 4 solutions	32

Instructions

- Time allowed for each paper: 1 hour.
- The maximum mark for each paper is 35 marks.
- You may NOT use a calculator for each paper.
- Attempt ALL questions.
- Full credit will be given only to solutions which contain appropriate working.
- Write your answers clearly in the spaces provided.
- State the units for your answer where appropriate.
- Unless otherwise stated in the question, all numerical answers should be given exactly or correct to three significant figures.
- Answers obtained by reading from scale drawing will not receive any credit.
- Use blue or black ink.

Paper 1   Non-Calculator

1. The complex numbers w and z satisfy the equations

    $w = 2zi$

    $\overline{w} + \overline{z} = 5 + 5i$

    Find w and z in the form $a + bi$ where $a, b \in \mathbb{Z}$. [4]

2. Use Gaussian elimination to solve the following system of equations. [4]

    $x + 2y - z = 2$

    $x - y + 2z = 5$

    $x + y + z = 6$

3. Matrix A is defined by $A = \begin{bmatrix} 2 & -3 \\ x & 5 \end{bmatrix}$, where $x \in \mathbb{R}$. Given that the determinant of A is 7, find:

   (a) the value of x; [3]

   (b) A^{-1}. [3]

4. (a) Given that $y = \dfrac{2 - 3x}{x^2 + 4}$, find $\dfrac{dy}{dx}$. Simplify your answer. [3]

   (b) Given that $f(x) = \sec 6x$, find $f'(x)$. [2]

5. Use the substitution $u = x^2 + 2$ to obtain $\int x(x^2 + 2)^4 dx$. [3]

6. Use the contrapositive to prove that if n^2 is even then n is even where $n \in \mathbb{Z}$. [3]

7. Find the area bounded by the curve $y = \dfrac{16}{x^2}$, the lines $y = 1$ and $y = 4$, and the y-axis. [5]

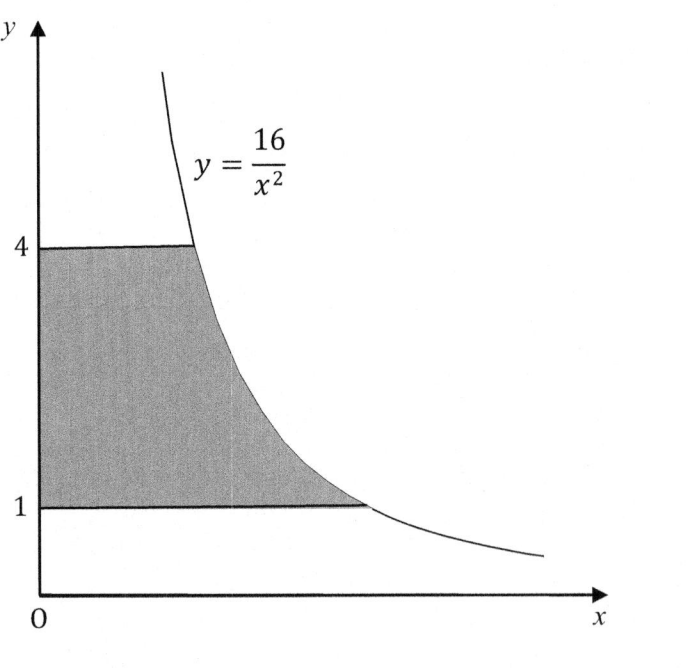

8. The area of a circular ink-blot on a sheet of blotting paper is increasing at a rate of $\dfrac{\pi}{4}$ cm² per second. Find the rate of increase of the radius of the ink-blot at the instant when its area is 4π cm². [5]

Paper 2 Non-Calculator

1. z is the complex number which satisfies the equation $3z - 4\bar{z} = 18 + 21i$.

   Find $\left|\dfrac{z}{3}\right|$. [3]

2. Use Gaussian elimination to show that the following system of equations is inconsistent. [3]

   $x + y - 2z = 3$

   $3x - 2y + 4z = 1$

   $2x - 3y + 6z = 10$

3. Matrix A is defined by $A = \begin{bmatrix} 3 & \lambda & -2 \\ 1 & 0 & 2 \\ -1 & 3 & 2 \end{bmatrix}$.

   (a) For what value of λ is A singular? [2]

   (b) State A'. [2]

4. (a) Given that $f(x) = x^2 e^{2x+3}$, find $f'(x)$. [2]

   (b) Given that $f(x) = \operatorname{cosec} x \ln(\sin x)$, find $f'(x)$, where $0 < x < \dfrac{\pi}{2}$. [2]

5. Use integration by parts to find $\int \ln x \, dx$. [2]

6. (a) On a single diagram, sketch the curve $y = 8x - x^2$ and the line $y = ax$, where $0 < a < 8$. [3]

(b) (i) Show that the area of the finite region enclosed between the curve and the line is $\dfrac{(8-a)^3}{6}$. [3]

(ii) Given that this area is exactly quarter the area enclosed between the curve and the *x*-axis, determine the exact value of *a* in the form $m + n\sqrt[3]{k}$, where *k*, *m* and *n* are integers. [3]

7. A 10 m long ladder is leaning against a wall. The bottom of the ladder starts to slip the floor at a rate of 0.2 m s^{-1}. Determine how fast the top of the ladder is moving down the wall at the instant when it is 8 m above the floor. [5]

8. Prove by induction that $\sum_{r=1}^{n} \frac{1}{r(r+1)} = \frac{n}{n+1}$ $\forall n \geq 1, n \in \mathbb{Z}$. [5]

Paper 3   Non-Calculator

1. Let $z = 3 - 2i$ and $w = -1 + i$.

    (a) Find $\dfrac{w}{z}$ in the form $a + bi$, where a and $b \in \mathbb{R}$. [2]

    (b) Find the real numbers p and q such that $pz + qw = 6$. [2]

2. Use Gaussian elimination to find the value of λ for which the following system of equations is inconsistent. [3]

    $x + 2y - 2z = 2$
    $3x + 4y - 5z = -3$
    $4x + 2y + \lambda z = -3$

3. Given that A is an invertible matrix given by $A = \begin{bmatrix} 1 & 1 & 2 \\ 2 & -2 & 3 \\ 4 & 2 & 8 \end{bmatrix}$, use elementary row operations to find A^{-1}. [3]

4. (a) Given that $f(x) = \cos^{-1} 3x$. Evaluate $f'\left(\dfrac{\sqrt{5}}{9}\right)$. [3]

(b) A curve is defined by the parametric equations
$x = 2t^3, y = t^2 + 3$
Find expressions for $\dfrac{dy}{dx}$ and $\dfrac{d^2y}{dx^2}$ in terms of t. [4]

5. Use partial fractions to find $\int \dfrac{x+16}{x^2+2x-8} dx$. [3]

6. The velocity of a particle, v m s^{-1}, at time t seconds is given by
$v = 0.3t^2 - 2.4t + 3.6$. The graph of v against t, for $0 \le t \le 8$, is shown below.

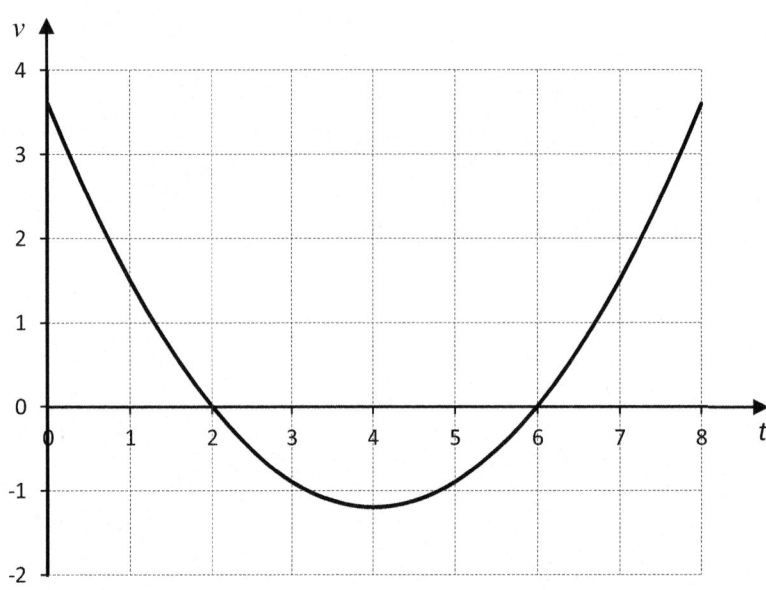

(a) What is the displacement of the particle from the starting position when $t = 3$ seconds? [2]

(b) Find the distance travelled by the particle in the first 3 seconds. [3]

7. (a) Find a counterexample to show that the following conjecture is false.

If $n \in \mathbb{Z}$ and n^2 is divisible by 4, then n is divisible by 4. [2]

(b) Prove directly that the sum of the squares of any two consecutive integers is odd. [2]

8. A function is defined on a suitable domain by $f(x) = \dfrac{x^2}{x^2 - 4}$.

(a) Obtain equations for the asymptotes of the graph of $y = f(x)$. [3]

(b) Determine whether the graph of $y = f(x)$ has any points of inflection. Justify your answer. [3]

Paper 4   Non-Calculator

1. The complex number $z = 1 - 2i$ is a root of the equation $z^3 + z^2 - z + p = 0$. Find the value of p and the remaining roots. [3]

2. (a) Use Gaussian elimination to find the value of λ for which the following system of equations has an infinite number of solutions. [3]

   $x + y + z = 2$

   $x - 3y - z = -4$

   $2x + 6y + \lambda z = 10$

   (b) Find x, y and z in terms of parameter t when λ takes this value. [2]

3. A non-singular $n \times n$ matrix A satisfies the equation $A^2 = 2A + 3I$, where I is the $n \times n$ identity matrix. Find the values of p and q for which $A^{-1} = pA + qI$. [2]

4. (a) Given that $y = 5^{x^2+1}$, find $\dfrac{dy}{dx}$ in terms of x. [3]

   (b) Given that $xy - x^3 + 2 = 0$, find expressions for $\dfrac{dy}{dx}$ and $\dfrac{d^2y}{dx^2}$ in terms of x and y. [4]

5. Use the substitution $u = 4x^2 + 1$ to obtain $\displaystyle\int_0^{\frac{\sqrt{3}}{2}} 2x\sqrt{4x^2 + 1}\,dx$. [4]

6. Find the volume of the solid formed when the region between the two curves $f(x) = \dfrac{\sqrt{x}}{2}$ and $g(x) = \dfrac{x^2}{16}$ is rotated 2π about

(a) the x-axis; [3]

(b) the y-axis. [3]

7. Prove by contradiction that $\sqrt{2}$ is irrational. [3]

8. Find the Maclaurin expansion for $f(x) = e^{2x} \cos x$ as far as the terms in x^4. [5]

Paper 1 solutions

1. The complex numbers w and z satisfy the equations

   $w = 2zi$

   $\overline{w} + \overline{z} = 5 + 5i$

   Find w and z in the form $a + bi$ where $a, b \in \mathbb{Z}$. [4]

   $z = x + yi$, $w = -2y + 2xi$, $\overline{z} = x - yi$, $\overline{w} = -2y - 2xi$

   Substituting $\overline{z} = x - yi$ and $\overline{w} = -2y - 2xi$ into $\overline{w} + \overline{z} = 5 + 5i$

   $-2y - 2xi + x - yi = 5 + 5i \Rightarrow -2y + x - 2xi - yi = 5 + 5i \Rightarrow$

   $-2x - y = 5$ (1), $x - 2y = 5$ (2)

   Solve the above Eqs (1) and (2).

   $x = -1, y = -3$

   Therefore $z = -1 - 3i$, $w = -2y + 2xi = 6 - 2i$

2. Use Gaussian elimination to solve the following system of equations. [4]

   $x + 2y - z = 2$

   $x - y + 2z = 5$

   $x + y + z = 6$

   $\begin{bmatrix} 1 & 2 & -1 & | & 2 \\ 1 & -1 & 2 & | & 5 \\ 1 & 1 & 1 & | & 6 \end{bmatrix} \xrightarrow{\substack{R_2 - R_1 \to R_2 \\ R_3 - R_1 \to R_3}} \begin{bmatrix} 1 & 2 & -1 & | & 2 \\ 0 & -3 & 3 & | & 3 \\ 0 & -1 & 2 & | & 4 \end{bmatrix} \xrightarrow{3R_3 - R_2 \to R_3} \begin{bmatrix} 1 & 2 & -1 & | & 2 \\ 0 & -3 & 3 & | & 3 \\ 0 & 0 & 3 & | & 9 \end{bmatrix}$

   $\Rightarrow$ $3z = 9 \Rightarrow z = 3$

   $-3y + 3z = 3 \Rightarrow y = z - 1 \Rightarrow y = 3 - 1 = 2$

   $x + 2y - z = 2 \Rightarrow x = 2 + z - 2y \Rightarrow x = 2 + 3 - 2 \times 2 = 1$

3. Matrix A is defined by $A = \begin{bmatrix} 2 & -3 \\ x & 5 \end{bmatrix}$, where $x \in \mathbb{R}$. Given that the determinant of A is 7, find:

   (a) the value of x; [3]

   $\det A = 2 \times 5 - x \times (-3)$, $2 \times 5 - x \times (-3) = 7 \Rightarrow x = -1$

   (b) A^{-1}. [3]

   $A^{-1} = \dfrac{1}{\det A} \begin{bmatrix} 5 & 3 \\ 1 & 2 \end{bmatrix} = \dfrac{1}{7} \begin{bmatrix} 5 & 3 \\ 1 & 2 \end{bmatrix}$

4. (a) Given that $y = \dfrac{2 - 3x}{x^2 + 4}$, find $\dfrac{dy}{dx}$. Simplify your answer. [3]

$$\dfrac{dy}{dx} = \dfrac{-3(x^2 + 4) - (2 - 3x) \times 2x}{(x^2 + 4)^2} = \dfrac{3x^2 - 4x - 12}{(x^2 + 4)^2}$$

(b) Given that $f(x) = \sec 6x$, find $f'(x)$. [2]

$f'(x) = \sec 6x \tan 6x \times 6 = 6 \sec 6x \tan 6x$

5. Use the substitution $u = x^2 + 2$ to obtain $\displaystyle\int x(x^2 + 2)^4 dx$. [3]

$u = x^2 + 2 \Rightarrow du = 2xdx \Rightarrow \dfrac{du}{2} = xdx$

$$\int x(x^2 + 2)^4 dx = \int \dfrac{1}{2} u^4 du = \dfrac{1}{2} \times \dfrac{1}{5} u^5 + c = \dfrac{1}{10}(x^2 + 2)^5 + c$$

6. Use the contrapositive to prove that if n^2 is even then n is even where $n \in \mathbb{Z}$. [3]

Contrapositive: if n is odd then n^2 is odd.

$\Rightarrow n = 2k + 1, k \in \mathbb{Z}$

$\Rightarrow n^2 = (2k + 1)^2 = 4k^2 + 4k + 1 = 2(2k^2 + 2k) + 1$ which is odd number.

So the contrapositive statement is true, therefore the original statement is true.

7. Find the area bounded by the curve $y = \dfrac{16}{x^2}$, the lines $y = 1$ and $y = 4$, and the y-axis. [5]

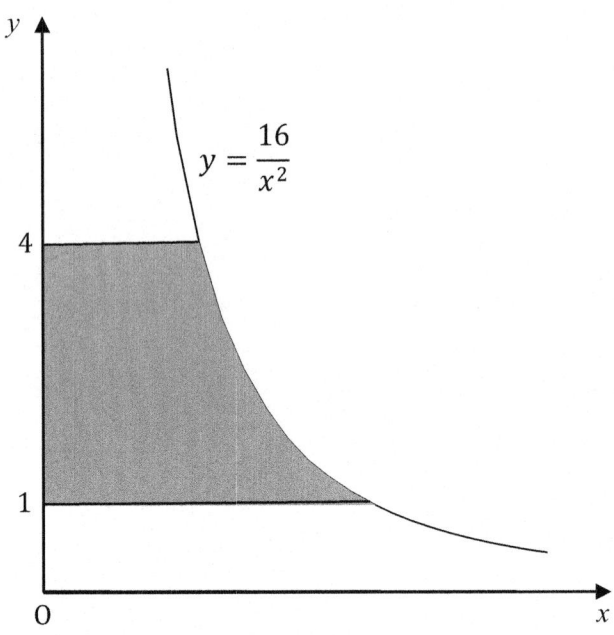

20

$$y = \frac{16}{x^2} \Rightarrow x = \frac{4}{\sqrt{y}}$$

$$A = \int_1^4 \frac{4}{\sqrt{y}} dy = \left[8\sqrt{y}\right]_1^4 = 8(\sqrt{4} - \sqrt{1}) = 8 \text{ square units}$$

8. The area of a circular ink-blot on a sheet of blotting paper is increasing at a rate of $\frac{\pi}{4}$ cm² per second. Find the rate of increase of the radius of the ink-blot at the instant when its area is 4π cm². [5]

$A = \pi r^2$

When $A = 4\pi, r = 2$.

$$\frac{dA}{dt} = 2\pi r \frac{dr}{dt} \Rightarrow \frac{dr}{dt} = \frac{1}{2\pi r}\frac{dA}{dt} = \frac{1}{2\pi \times 2} \times \frac{1}{4}\pi = \frac{1}{16}$$

The rate of increase of the radius of the ink-blot is $\frac{1}{16}$ cm per second at the instant when its area is 4π cm².

Paper 2 solutions

1. z is the complex number which satisfies the equation $3z - 4\bar{z} = 18 + 21i$.

   Find $\left|\frac{z}{3}\right|$. [3]

   $z = x + yi$

   $3z - 4\bar{z} = 18 + 21i \Rightarrow 3x + 3yi - 4x + 4yi = 18 + 21i \Rightarrow$

   $-x + 7yi = 18 + 21i \Rightarrow$

   $x = -18$

   $y = 3$

   $z = -18 + 3i$

   $\left|\frac{z}{3}\right| = |-6 + i| = \sqrt{6^2 + 1^2} = \sqrt{37}$

2. Use Gaussian elimination to show that the following system of equations is inconsistent. [3]

   $x + y - 2z = 3$

   $3x - 2y + 4z = 1$

   $2x - 3y + 6z = 10$

   $\begin{bmatrix} 1 & 1 & -2 & | & 3 \\ 3 & -2 & 4 & | & 1 \\ 2 & -3 & 6 & | & 10 \end{bmatrix} \xrightarrow[R_3 - 2R_1 \to R_3]{R_2 - 3R_1 \to R_2} \begin{bmatrix} 1 & 1 & -2 & | & 3 \\ 0 & -5 & 10 & | & -8 \\ 0 & -5 & 10 & | & 4 \end{bmatrix} \xrightarrow{R_3 - R_2 \to R_3} \begin{bmatrix} 1 & 1 & -2 & | & 3 \\ 0 & -5 & 10 & | & -8 \\ 0 & 0 & 0 & | & 12 \end{bmatrix}$

   $R_3: 0x + 0y + 0z = 12$ which is impossible, so the system of equations has no solution and is said to be inconsistent.

3. Matrix A is defined by $A = \begin{bmatrix} 3 & \lambda & -2 \\ 1 & 0 & 2 \\ -1 & 3 & 2 \end{bmatrix}$.

   (a) For what value of λ is A singular? [2]

   $\det A = 3\begin{vmatrix} 0 & 2 \\ 3 & 2 \end{vmatrix} - \lambda\begin{vmatrix} 1 & 2 \\ -1 & 2 \end{vmatrix} - 2\begin{vmatrix} 1 & 0 \\ -1 & 3 \end{vmatrix} = -18 - 4\lambda - 6$

   $\det A = 0 \Rightarrow -18 - 4\lambda - 6 = 0 \Rightarrow \lambda = -6$

   When $\lambda = -6$, A is singular.

   (b) State A'. [2]

   $A' = \begin{bmatrix} 3 & 1 & -1 \\ \lambda & 0 & 3 \\ -2 & 2 & 2 \end{bmatrix}$

4. (a) Given that $f(x) = x^2 e^{2x+3}$, find $f'(x)$. [2]

$f'(x) = 2xe^{2x+3} + x^2 e^{2x+3} \times 2 = 2xe^{2x+3}(1+x)$

(b) Given that $f(x) = \operatorname{cosec} x \ln(\sin x)$, find $f'(x)$, where $0 < x < \dfrac{\pi}{2}$. [2]

$f'(x) = -\operatorname{cosec} x \cot x \ln(\sin x) + \operatorname{cosec} x \times \dfrac{\cos x}{\sin x} = \operatorname{cosec} x \cot x \,(1 - \ln(\sin x))$

5. Use integration by parts to find $\displaystyle\int \ln x \, dx$. [2]

$f(x) = \ln x \Rightarrow f'(x) = \dfrac{1}{x}; \ g(x) = x \Rightarrow g'(x) = 1$

$\displaystyle\int \ln x \, dx = x \ln x - \int x \times \dfrac{1}{x} dx = x \ln x - x + c = x(\ln x - 1) + c$

6. (a) On a single diagram, sketch the curve $y = 8x - x^2$ and the line $y = ax$, where $0 < a < 8$. [3]

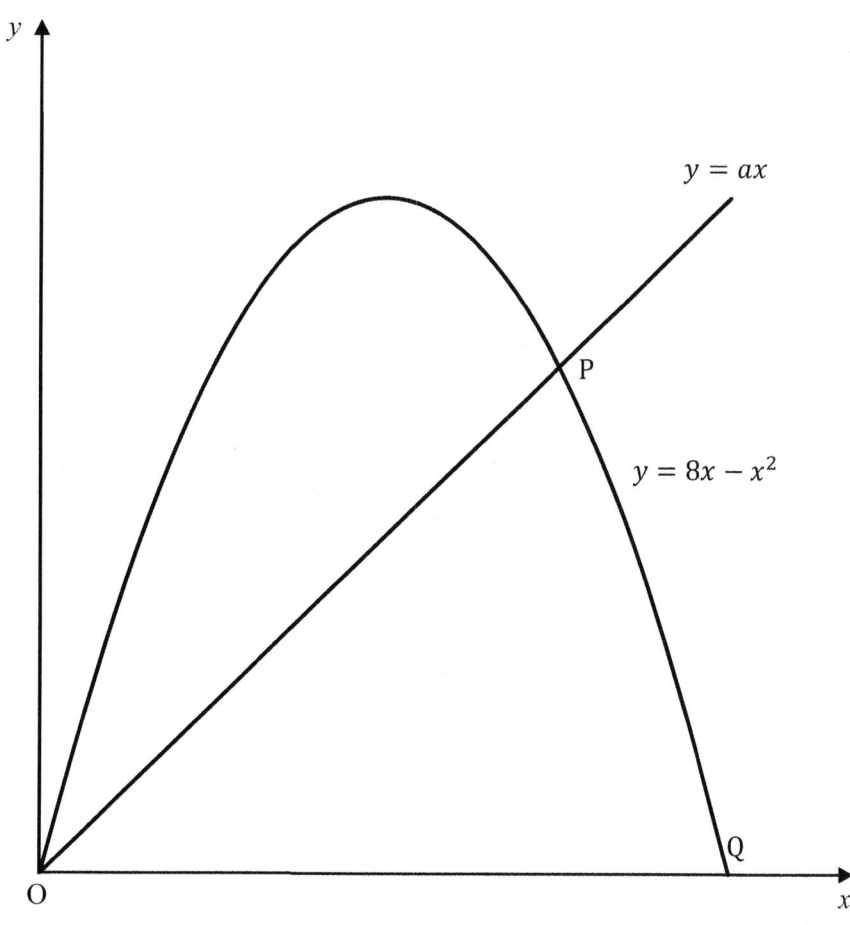

(b) (i) Show that the area of the finite region enclosed between the curve and the line is $\frac{(8-a)^3}{6}$. [3]

The line $y = ax$ intersects the curve at point P. The x-coordinate of point P can be calculated as follows:

$ax = 8x - x^2 \Rightarrow x(x + a - 8) = 0$

Therefore the x-coordinate of point P is $8 - a$

The area of the finite region enclosed between the curve and the line can be calculated as follows:

$$\int_0^{8-a} ((8x - x^2) - ax)dx = \int_0^{8-a} ((8-a)x - x^2)dx = \left[\frac{8-a}{2}x^2 - \frac{x^3}{3}\right]_0^{8-a}$$

$$= \frac{(8-a)^3}{2} - \frac{(8-a)^3}{3} = \frac{(8-a)^3}{6}$$

(ii) Given that this area is exactly quarter the area enclosed between the curve and the x-axis, determine the exact value of a in the form $m + n\sqrt[3]{k}$, where k, m and n are integers. [3]

The x-axis intersects the curve at point $Q(8, 0)$.

The area enclosed between the curve and the x-axis is:

$$\int_0^8 (8x - x^2)dx = \left[4x^2 - \frac{x^3}{3}\right]_0^8 = \left[\frac{x^2(12 - x)}{3}\right]_0^8 = \frac{64 \times 4}{3}$$

$$\frac{4 \times (8-a)^3}{6} = \frac{64 \times 4}{3} \Rightarrow (8-a)^3 = 2 \times 64 \Rightarrow 8 - a = 4\sqrt[3]{2} \Rightarrow a = 8 - 4\sqrt[3]{2}$$

7. A 10 m long ladder is leaning against a wall. The bottom of the ladder starts to slip the floor at a rate of 0.2 m s^{-1}. Determine how fast the top of the ladder is moving down the wall at the instant when it is 8 m above the floor. [5]

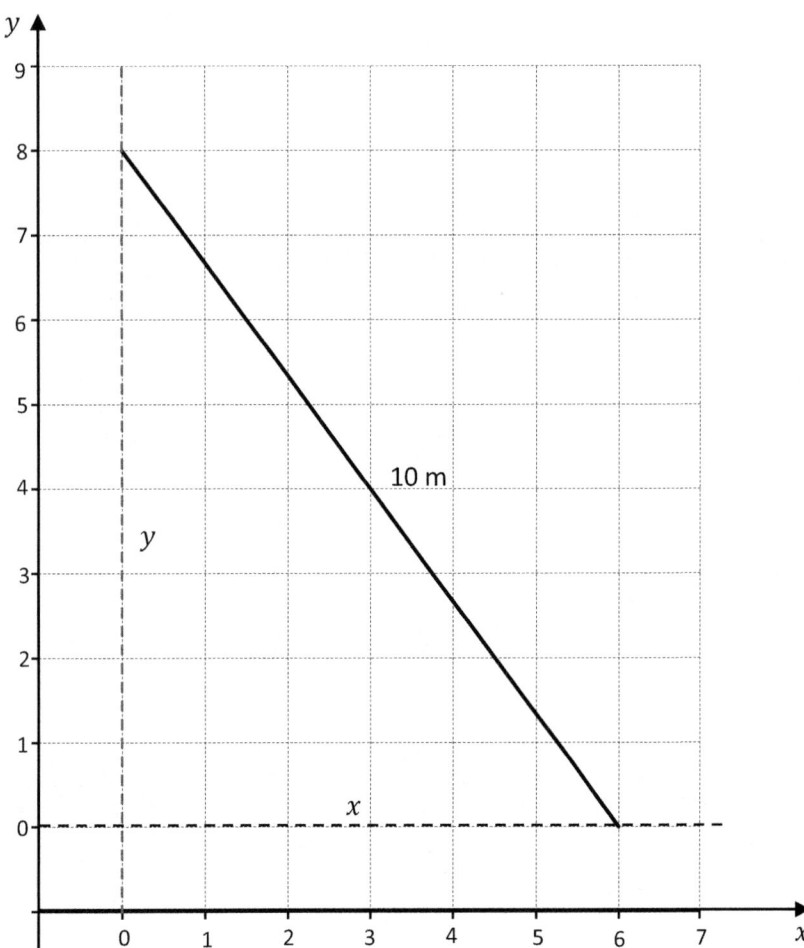

$x^2 + y^2 = 100$

$2x\dfrac{dx}{dt} + 2y\dfrac{dy}{dt} = 0$

$y = 8; \; x = \sqrt{100 - 8^2} = 6; \; \dfrac{dx}{dt} = 0.2$

$\dfrac{dy}{dt} = -\dfrac{x}{y}\dfrac{dx}{dt} = -\dfrac{6}{8} \times 0.2 = -0.15$

The top of the ladder is moving down the wall at 0.15 m per second at the instant when it is 8 m above the floor.

8. Prove by induction that $\sum_{r=1}^{n} \frac{1}{r(r+1)} = \frac{n}{n+1}$ $\forall n \geq 1, n \in \mathbb{Z}$. [5]

When $n = 1$, LHS $= \frac{1}{1 \times (1+1)} = \frac{1}{2}$, RHS $= \frac{1}{1+1} = \frac{1}{2}$; so true when $n = 1$.

Assume true for $n = k$, i.e.

$$\sum_{r=1}^{k} \frac{1}{r(r+1)} = \frac{k}{k+1}$$

When $n = k + 1$

$$\text{LHS} = \sum_{r=1}^{k+1} \frac{1}{r(r+1)} = \sum_{r=1}^{k} \frac{1}{r(r+1)} + \frac{1}{(k+1)(k+2)} = \frac{k}{k+1} + \frac{1}{(k+1)(k+2)}$$

$$= \frac{k(k+2)+1}{(k+1)(k+2)} = \frac{(k+1)^2}{(k+1)(k+2)} = \frac{k+1}{k+2}$$

RHS $= \frac{k+1}{k+2}$

∴ if true for $n = k$, then also true for $n = k + 1$. So, since also true for $n = 1$ then, by induction, true for $\forall n \geq 1, n \in \mathbb{Z}$.

Paper 3 solutions

1. Let $z = 3 - 2i$ and $w = -1 + i$.

   (a) Find $\dfrac{w}{z}$ in the form $a + bi$, where a and $b \in \mathbb{R}$. [2]

   $$\frac{w}{z} = \frac{-1+i}{3-2i} = \frac{(-1+i)(3+2i)}{(3-2i)(3+2i)} = \frac{-3+i-2}{9+4} = -\frac{5}{13} + \frac{1}{13}i$$

   (b) Find the real numbers p and q such that $pz + qw = 6$. [2]

   $p(3 - 2i) + q(-1 + i) = 6 \Rightarrow 3p - q + i(-2p + q) = 6$

   $-2p + q = 0$ \hfill (1)

   $3p - q = 6$ \hfill (2)

   Eq. (1) $\Rightarrow q = 2p$ \hfill (3)

   Eqs. (2) and (3) $\Rightarrow 3p - 2p = 6 \Rightarrow p = 6, q = 12$

2. Use Gaussian elimination to find the value of λ for which the following system of equations is inconsistent. [3]

   $x + 2y - 2z = 2$

   $3x + 4y - 5z = -3$

   $4x + 2y + \lambda z = -3$

   $$\begin{bmatrix} 1 & 2 & -2 & | & 2 \\ 3 & 4 & -5 & | & -3 \\ 4 & 2 & \lambda & | & -3 \end{bmatrix} \xrightarrow{\substack{R_2 - 3R_1 \to R_2 \\ R_3 - 4R_1 \to R_3}} \begin{bmatrix} 1 & 1 & -2 & | & 2 \\ 0 & -2 & 1 & | & -9 \\ 0 & -6 & \lambda+8 & | & -11 \end{bmatrix} \xrightarrow{R_3 - 3R_2 \to R_3} \begin{bmatrix} 1 & 1 & -2 & | & 2 \\ 0 & -2 & 1 & | & -9 \\ 0 & 0 & \lambda+5 & | & 16 \end{bmatrix}$$

   The system of equations is inconsistent when $\lambda + 5 = 0$, i.e. when $\lambda = -5$.

3. Given that A is an invertible matrix given by $A = \begin{bmatrix} 1 & 1 & 2 \\ 2 & -2 & 3 \\ 4 & 2 & 8 \end{bmatrix}$, use elementary row operations to find A^{-1}. [3]

$\begin{bmatrix} 1 & 1 & 2 & | & 1 & 0 & 0 \\ 2 & -2 & 3 & | & 0 & 1 & 0 \\ 4 & 2 & 8 & | & 0 & 0 & 1 \end{bmatrix} \xrightarrow{\substack{R_2-2R_1 \to R_2 \\ R_3-4R_1 \to R_3}} \begin{bmatrix} 1 & 1 & 2 & | & 1 & 0 & 0 \\ 0 & -4 & -1 & | & -2 & 1 & 0 \\ 0 & -2 & 0 & | & -4 & 0 & 1 \end{bmatrix} \xrightarrow{R_2-2R_3 \to R_2}$

$\begin{bmatrix} 1 & 1 & 2 & | & 1 & 0 & 0 \\ 0 & 0 & -1 & | & 6 & 1 & -2 \\ 0 & -2 & 0 & | & -4 & 0 & 1 \end{bmatrix} \xrightarrow{R_1+\frac{1}{2}R_3 \to R_1} \begin{bmatrix} 1 & 0 & 2 & | & -1 & 0 & \frac{1}{2} \\ 0 & 0 & -1 & | & 6 & 1 & -2 \\ 0 & -2 & 0 & | & -4 & 0 & 1 \end{bmatrix} \xrightarrow{R_1+2R_2 \to R_1}$

$\begin{bmatrix} 1 & 0 & 0 & | & 11 & 2 & -\frac{7}{2} \\ 0 & 0 & -1 & | & 6 & 1 & -2 \\ 0 & -2 & 0 & | & -4 & 0 & 1 \end{bmatrix} \xrightarrow{\substack{-R_2 \to R_2 \\ -\frac{1}{2}R_3 \to R_3}} \begin{bmatrix} 1 & 0 & 0 & | & 11 & 2 & -\frac{7}{2} \\ 0 & 0 & 1 & | & -6 & -1 & 2 \\ 0 & 1 & 0 & | & 2 & 0 & -\frac{1}{2} \end{bmatrix} \xrightarrow{R_2 \leftrightarrow R_3}$

$\begin{bmatrix} 1 & 0 & 0 & | & 11 & 2 & -\frac{7}{2} \\ 0 & 1 & 0 & | & 2 & 0 & -\frac{1}{2} \\ 0 & 0 & 1 & | & -6 & -1 & 2 \end{bmatrix} \Rightarrow A^{-1} = \begin{bmatrix} 11 & 2 & -\frac{7}{2} \\ 2 & 0 & -\frac{1}{2} \\ -6 & -1 & 2 \end{bmatrix}$

4. (a) Given that $f(x) = \cos^{-1} 3x$. Evaluate $f'\left(\frac{\sqrt{5}}{9}\right)$. [3]

$f'(x) = -\dfrac{3}{\sqrt{1-9x^2}}$

$f'\left(\dfrac{\sqrt{5}}{9}\right) = -\dfrac{3}{\sqrt{1-9\times\left(\frac{\sqrt{5}}{9}\right)^2}} = -\dfrac{3}{\sqrt{1-\frac{5}{9}}} = -\dfrac{3}{\frac{2}{3}} = -\dfrac{9}{2}$

(b) A curve is defined by the parametric equations
$x = 2t^3, y = t^2 + 3$
Find expressions for $\dfrac{dy}{dx}$ and $\dfrac{d^2y}{dx^2}$ in terms of t. [4]

$\dfrac{dx}{dt} = 6t^2, \dfrac{dy}{dt} = 2t \Rightarrow \dfrac{dy}{dx} = \dfrac{2t}{6t^2} = \dfrac{1}{3t}$

$\dfrac{d^2y}{dx^2} = \dfrac{d}{dt}\left(\dfrac{dy}{dx}\right)\dfrac{dt}{dx} = -\dfrac{1}{3t^2} \times \dfrac{1}{6t^2} = -\dfrac{1}{18t^4}$

5. Use partial fractions to find $\int \frac{x+16}{x^2+2x-8} dx$. [3]

$\frac{x+16}{x^2+2x-8} = \frac{x+16}{(x-2)(x+4)} = \frac{A}{x-2} + \frac{B}{x+4} = \frac{A(x+4)+B(x-2)}{(x-2)(x+4)} \Rightarrow$

$A(x+4) + B(x-2) = x+16$ \hfill (1)

Substituting $x = 2$ into Eq. (1) gives $6A = 18 \Rightarrow A = 3$

Substituting $x = -4$ into Eq. (1) gives $-6B = 12 \Rightarrow B = -2$

$\int \frac{x+16}{x^2+2x-8} dx = \int \left(\frac{3}{x-2} - \frac{2}{x+4}\right) dx = 3\ln|x-2| - 2\ln|x+4| + c$

$= \ln\left|\frac{(x-2)^3}{(x+4)^2}\right| + c$

6. The velocity of a particle, v m s^{-1}, at time t seconds is given by

$v = 0.3t^2 - 2.4t + 3.6$. The graph of v against t, for $0 \leq t \leq 8$, is shown below.

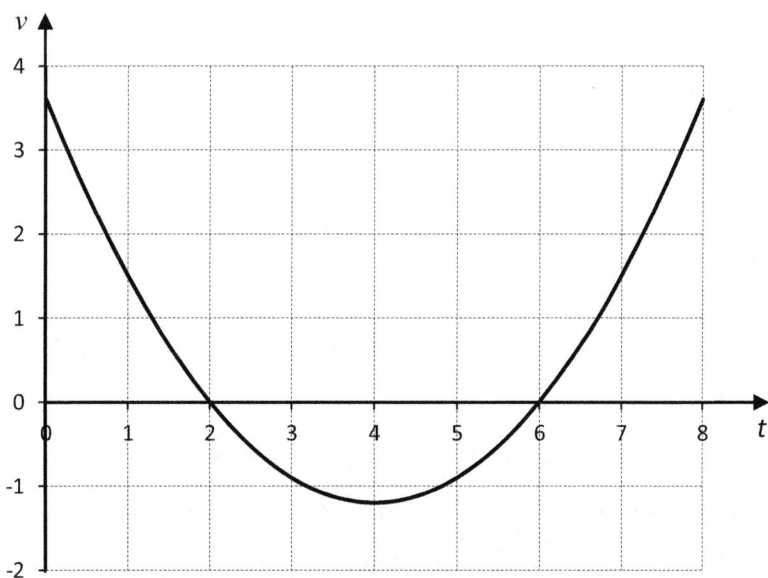

(a) What is the displacement of the particle from the starting position when $t = 3$ seconds? [2]

$\int_0^3 (0.3t^2 - 2.4t + 3.6) dt = [0.1t^3 - 1.2t^2 + 3.6t]_0^3 = 2.7$ m

(b) Find the distance travelled by the particle in the first 3 seconds. [3]

$$\int_0^2 (0.3t^2 - 2.4t + 3.6)dt - \int_2^3 (0.3t^2 - 2.4t + 3.6)dt$$

$$= \int_0^2 (0.3t^2 - 2.4t + 3.6)dt - \int_0^3 (0.3t^2 - 2.4t + 3.6)dt$$

$$+ \int_0^2 (0.3t^2 - 2.4t + 3.6)dt$$

$$= 2\int_0^2 (0.3t^2 - 2.4t + 3.6)dt - \int_0^3 (0.3t^2 - 2.4t + 3.6)dt$$

$$= 2[0.1t^3 - 1.2t^2 + 3.6t]_0^2 - [0.1t^3 - 1.2t^2 + 3.6t]_0^3 = 3.7 \text{ m}$$

7. (a) Find a counterexample to show that the following conjecture is false.

If $n \in \mathbb{Z}$ and n^2 is divisible by 4, then n is divisible by 4. [2]

When $n = 6$, $n^2 = 36$ which is divisible by 4, but 6 is not divisible by 4.

(b) Prove directly that the sum of the squares of any two consecutive integers is odd. [2]

Let the numbers be n and $n + 1$ where $n \in \mathbb{Z}$.

$n^2 + (n + 1)^2 = n^2 + n^2 + 2n + 1 = 2(n^2 + n) + 1$

$2(n^2 + n) + 1$ is old, therefore the sum of the squares of any two consecutive integers is odd.

8. A function is defined on a suitable domain by $f(x) = \dfrac{x^2}{x^2 - 4}$.

(a) Obtain equations for the asymptotes of the graph of $y = f(x)$. [3]

$$f(x) = \frac{x^2}{x^2 - 4} = \frac{x^2 - 4 + 4}{x^2 - 4} = 1 + \frac{4}{x^2 - 4} = 1 + \frac{4}{(x-2)(x+2)}$$

$x = 2$ and $x = -2$ are vertical asymptotes.

$f(x) \to 1$ as $x \to \pm\infty$, so $y = 1$ is a horizontal asymptote.

(b) Determine whether the graph of $y = f(x)$ has any points of inflection. Justify your answer. [3]

$$f'(x) = \frac{2x(x^2 - 4) - 2x \times x^2}{(x^2 - 4)^2} = -\frac{8x}{(x^2 - 4)^2}$$

$$f''(x) = -\frac{8(x^2 - 4)^2 - 8x \times 2(x^2 - 4) \times 2x}{(x^2 - 4)^4} = \frac{32 + 24x^2}{(x^2 - 4)^3} \neq 0$$

$f''(x)$ is undefined only when $x = \pm 2$. Since $f(x)$ is undefined at these values, there is no point of inflection.

Paper 4 solutions

1. The complex number $z = 1 - 2i$ is a root of the equation $z^3 + z^2 - z + p = 0$. Find the value of p and the remaining roots. [3]

   $z = 1 - 2i$ is a root, so $z = 1 + 2i$ is also a root. Let $z = b$ is the third root.
   $(z - 1 + 2i)(z - 1 - 2i)(z - b) = z^3 + z^2 - z + p \Rightarrow$
   $(z^2 - 2z + 5)(z - b) = z^3 + z^2 - z + p \Rightarrow$
   $z^3 - (2 + b)z^2 + (5 + 2b)z - 5b = z^3 + z^2 - z + p \Rightarrow$
   $b = -3, p = 15$

   Therefore the remaining roots are -3, $1 + 2i$, and the value of p is 15.

2. (a) Use Gaussian elimination to find the value of λ for which the following system of equations has an infinite number of solutions. [3]

   $x + y + z = 2$
   $x - 3y - z = -4$
   $2x + 6y + \lambda z = 10$

   $\begin{bmatrix} 1 & 1 & 1 & | & 2 \\ 1 & -3 & -1 & | & -4 \\ 2 & 6 & \lambda & | & 10 \end{bmatrix} \xrightarrow{\substack{R_2-R_1 \to R_2 \\ R_3-2R_1 \to R_3}} \begin{bmatrix} 1 & 1 & 1 & | & 2 \\ 0 & -4 & -2 & | & -6 \\ 0 & 4 & \lambda-2 & | & 6 \end{bmatrix} \xrightarrow{R_3+R_2 \to R_3} \begin{bmatrix} 1 & 1 & 1 & | & 2 \\ 0 & -4 & -2 & | & -6 \\ 0 & 0 & \lambda-4 & | & 0 \end{bmatrix}$

   $\Rightarrow \lambda - 4 = 0 \Rightarrow \lambda = 4$

   (b) Find x, y and z in terms of parameter t when λ takes this value. [2]

   Let $z = t, \lambda = 4$

   $-4y - 2z = -6 \Rightarrow 2y + z = 3 \Rightarrow y = \dfrac{3-z}{2} \Rightarrow y = \dfrac{3-t}{2}$

   $x + y + z = 2 \Rightarrow x = 2 - y - z \Rightarrow x = 2 - \dfrac{3-t}{2} - t \Rightarrow x = \dfrac{1-t}{2}$

3. A non-singular $n \times n$ matrix A satisfies the equation $A^2 = 2A + 3I$, where I is the $n \times n$ identity matrix. Find the values of p and q for which $A^{-1} = pA + qI$. [2]

   $A^2 = 2A + 3I \Rightarrow A^2 A^{-1} = 2AA^{-1} + 3IA^{-1} \Rightarrow A = 2I + 3A^{-1} \Rightarrow A^{-1} = \dfrac{A - 2I}{3} \Rightarrow$

   $p = \dfrac{1}{3}, q = -\dfrac{2}{3}$

4. (a) Given that $y = 5^{x^2+1}$, find $\dfrac{dy}{dx}$ in terms of x. [3]

$y = 5^{x^2+1} \Rightarrow \ln y = (x^2+1)\ln 5 \Rightarrow \dfrac{1}{y}\dfrac{dy}{dx} = 2x\ln 5 \Rightarrow \dfrac{dy}{dx} = 2xy\ln 5 \Rightarrow$

$\dfrac{dy}{dx} = 2x 5^{x^2+1}\ln 5 = (10\ln 5)5^{x^2}x$

(b) Given that $xy - x^3 + 2 = 0$, find expressions for $\dfrac{dy}{dx}$ and $\dfrac{d^2y}{dx^2}$ in terms of x and y. [4]

$y + x\dfrac{dy}{dx} - 3x^2 = 0 \Rightarrow \dfrac{dy}{dx} = \dfrac{3x^2 - y}{x}$

$\dfrac{d^2y}{dx^2} = \dfrac{\left(6x - \dfrac{dy}{dx}\right)x - (3x^2 - y)}{x^2} = \dfrac{3x^2 + y - x\dfrac{3x^2 - y}{x}}{x^2} = \dfrac{2y}{x^2}$

5. Use the substitution $u = 4x^2 + 1$ to obtain $\displaystyle\int_0^{\frac{\sqrt{3}}{2}} 2x\sqrt{4x^2+1}\,dx$. [4]

$u = 4x^2 + 1 \Rightarrow du = 8x\,dx$

$x = \dfrac{\sqrt{3}}{2} \Rightarrow u = 4 \times \left(\dfrac{\sqrt{3}}{2}\right)^2 + 1 = 4$

$x = 0 \Rightarrow u = 4 \times (0)^2 + 1 = 1$

$\displaystyle\int_0^{\frac{\sqrt{3}}{2}} 2x\sqrt{4x^2+1}\,dx = \dfrac{1}{4}\int_0^{\frac{\sqrt{3}}{2}} 8x\sqrt{4x^2+1}\,dx = \dfrac{1}{4}\int_1^4 \sqrt{u}\,du = \dfrac{1}{4}\left[\dfrac{2u^{\frac{3}{2}}}{3}\right]_1^4$

$= \dfrac{1}{6} \times 4^{\frac{3}{2}} - \dfrac{1}{6} \times 1^{\frac{3}{2}} = \dfrac{8}{6} - \dfrac{1}{6} = \dfrac{7}{6}$

6. Find the volume of the solid formed when the region between the two curves $f(x) = \dfrac{\sqrt{x}}{2}$ and $g(x) = \dfrac{x^2}{16}$ is rotated 2π about

(a) the x-axis; [3]

Sketch the graphs and find the points of intersection.

33

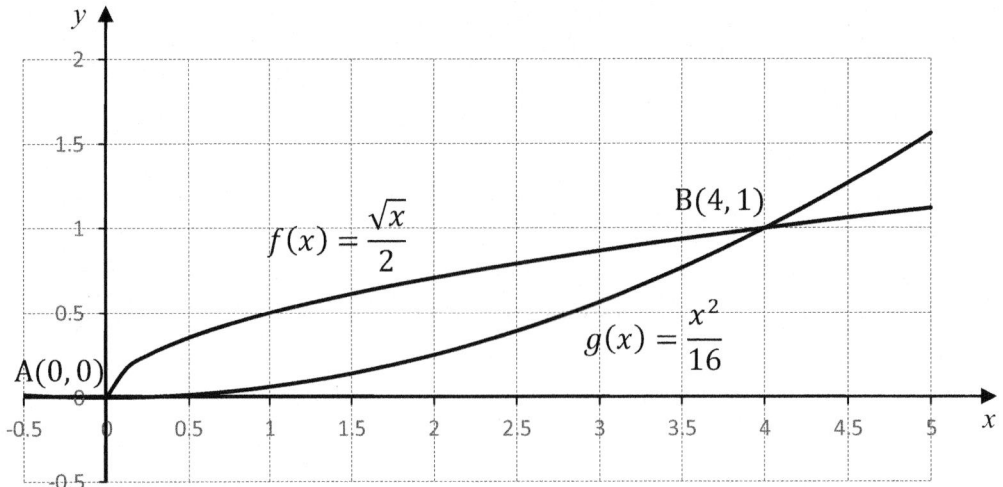

$$V = \pi \int_0^4 \left((f(x))^2 - (g(x))^2\right) dx = \pi \int_0^4 \left(\left(\frac{\sqrt{x}}{2}\right)^2 - \left(\frac{x^2}{16}\right)^2\right) dx$$

$$= \pi \int_0^4 \left(\frac{x}{4} - \frac{x^4}{16 \times 16}\right) dx = \pi \left[\frac{x^2}{8} - \frac{x^5}{5 \times 16 \times 16}\right]_0^4 = \pi \left(2 - \frac{4}{5}\right) = \frac{6\pi}{5} \text{ cubic units}$$

(b)   the *y*-axis. [3]

$$f(x) = \frac{\sqrt{x}}{2}, x = 4y^2$$

$$g(x) = \frac{x^2}{16}, x = 4\sqrt{y}$$

$$V = \pi \int_0^1 \left((4\sqrt{y})^2 - (4y^2)^2\right) dy = \pi \int_0^1 (16y - 16y^4) dy = 16\pi \left[\frac{y^2}{2} - \frac{y^5}{5}\right]_0^1$$

$$= 16\pi \left(\frac{1}{2} - \frac{1}{5}\right) = \frac{24\pi}{5} \text{ cubic units}$$

7. Prove by contradiction that $\sqrt{2}$ is irrational. [3]

Assume that $\sqrt{2}$ is rational, then $\sqrt{2} = \dfrac{m}{n}$ where $m, n \in \mathbb{Z}$ and m, n have no common factors.

$$\Rightarrow 2 = \frac{m^2}{n^2} \Rightarrow m^2 = 2n^2$$

This means that m is an even integer.

$$\Rightarrow m = 2k \Rightarrow m^2 = 4k^2$$

This leads to:

$$m^2 = 4k^2 = 2n^2 \Rightarrow n^2 = 2k^2$$

This means that n is also an even integer. m, n have a common factor of 2. This contradicts the assumption, hence the original statement is true.

8. Find the Maclaurin expansion for $f(x) = e^{2x} \cos x$ as far as the terms in x^4. [5]

$$e^x = 1 + x + \frac{x^2}{2!} + \frac{x^3}{3!} + \frac{x^4}{4!} + \cdots$$

$$e^{2x} = 1 + (2x) + \frac{(2x)^2}{2!} + \frac{(2x)^3}{3!} + \frac{(2x)^4}{4!} + \cdots = 1 + 2x + 2x^2 + \frac{4x^3}{3} + \frac{2x^4}{3} + \cdots$$

$$\cos x = 1 - \frac{x^2}{2!} + \frac{x^4}{4!} + \cdots$$

$$e^{2x} \cos x = \left(1 + 2x + 2x^2 + \frac{4x^3}{3} + \frac{2x^4}{3} + \cdots\right)\left(1 - \frac{x^2}{2!} + \frac{x^4}{4!} + \cdots\right)$$

$$\approx \left(1 + 2x + 2x^2 + \frac{4x^3}{3} + \frac{2x^4}{3}\right) - \frac{x^2}{2!}(1 + 2x + 2x^2) + \frac{x^4}{4!}$$

$$= 1 + 2x + \frac{3x^2}{2} + \frac{x^3}{3} - \frac{7x^4}{24}$$

Printed in Great Britain
by Amazon